WITCHDOCTORPOET

I hope these words
remind you that
you are magical
beyond measure.
Wishing you a
magical journey
of healing +
self-discovery.

for Mom
for G
In memory of Baba
In memory of tomorrow

offerings

Noose
The Favorite Daughter
Burning
Sun Scab
Scolding Spirits
When A Parent Leaves
The Addict Within
Frail
First Kiss
Niger Delta Meets Flint
Silenced
The Broken Heart
The Art of Raising a Blade
Anger: The Perfume My Skin Wears
Speak
Babble
My Demons & I

<u>the root work</u>

Igbo Landing
Questions
Grandpa v. Jim Crow
Heirloom
Alternative Reality | Simulator
Lies
Wound Cleaning
Middle Passage (I) & (II)
EPSOM SALT & LAVENDER
The Landfill of Bones
Weeping Through Moonset Eyes
Desire
Milk
Standing in Our Power
I + I
  ()
Kintsugi

the worship

lost souls

W ill you kick the chair

from underneath me ?

I want to *fly*

                    Noose -

D-d walks out of the room
whenever I mention G-d

*"Must be nice creating a world
you don't have to live in"*

He surrenders his head back
chugging down spoiled nectar
until his eyes glaze over

While he is asleep
I grab the beer bottle by its neck

Why is she his favorite?

Yes, I carry D-d's face
but she ...
she seeps from his pores

9

Burning

A phoenix
is only as fierce as the ashes it crawls out of

Sun Scab

I.

The sun is a scab that won't leave my bones
I'd scrub her off my knee caps
but she'd find a way to pour back in

II.

A small boy points me out in the darkness
Negra Fea
Mira, una negra fea!

My spirit folds herself in half

III.

The beauty supply owner follows me around his shop

He does skin readings
pointing at the hue in my 'suspicious' face

"The sun put a hex on you" he says
placing a jar of bleaching cream on the counter

I hand over a folded dollar bill
He holds it up to the light
impressed by the hologram of Andrew Jackson's face

IV.

I 've mapped out how to outshadow my shadow
I keep spare umbrellas in my bag in case the sun
comes out swinging

Before bed
I hold a pocket knife to my face and watch my smile
spread wide like the girls on the relaxer cream box

My soul nods off with her eyes wide open
in my dreams is where she'll feel beautiful

Scolding Spirits

My throat holds a corridor of spirits
they ask why I never use their voices
and why has my own gone numb?

I tell them
The world loves me best quiet

They laugh
spilling rum out of the corners of their mouths

Honey, that doesn't sound like love at all!

Turn around,

look me in the face
tell me I'm not yours

I'll listen
this time
I'll listen

-     *when a parent leaves*

The Addict Within

My soul returns home drunk
bowing her head like a sinner saying grace

Behind her eyelids is an afterlife of
ghosts
I wail from the base of my throat
begging my soul not to return to them

Who am I to blame her ?

How is G-d to blame her ?

Is it not us who drag her
through the weight
of a body she never asked for?

Frail

A synonym for human is "frail"

why is that?

why do we forget
it takes strength to carry this body
through an unforgiving world

First Kiss

Jacob's tongue was
a python swallowing the wide of my mouth
we held our breaths forever
or at least until our eyes ran mad

Jamal - his eldest brother
had a scent that was fresh on my mind

abeg
abeg
and I kept begging for air

What was that feeling under my skirt
and which one of them put it there?

Niger Delta Meets Flint

They found me floating facedown
draining pulp from the river's belly

The river and I are kinfolk
both fistula and rot
both open wet things men with oars paddle through

Fishermen once pulled up cocoyam,

pumpkin, and a handful of mirrors
Now their nets cough up corpses
with eyes that leak tar

My children sink their teeth into the river's mouth and

pull up blood
They go weeks without water
washing their mouths with the crudest oil: *reality*

Notice how they never flinch when they glare at the sky

"It is the sun who witnesses all but does nothing"

They roam the streets with hands balled into fists
Even though
I've warned them many times not to pick a fight with G-d

Silenced

I wear many faces

Some drip when wet
others foam at the corners of their mouths

Don't be fooled
I know how to
feign happiness

look closely

My eyes are swollen
with an honesty
my lips can't express

The Broken Heart

I'm a new shade of nude
anointed with a face my elders
can't even recognize

The Art of Raising a Blade

Do you see your son?
Look at how he scars his face as he shaves

He stares into the mirror
pointing out the parts of you that couldn't run away

He raises a blade to his neck
chanting your name three times

You never appear
but his inner demons do

Online

he researches
"How to tie a tie"

for dances
for dates
for interviews
~~for suicide attempts~~

For the pain of
searching for a f-ther
who is a ghost at best
and a haunting at worst

Anger: The Perfume My Skin Wears

*A*nger carries many faces
yet wears the same stale cologne

She waddles through neighborhoods
in a bloodstained battledress
Her eyes flared
Her lips oozing something vile

If you ask her whose blood she wears
She'll point at me

Speak

You smell violent
when you make your
heart hold its tongue

Babble

When seeds get old enough
We start teething
Our voices roar as we
back-talk ourselves out of smallness

Devils run after
our blossoming breath
and demand we "quiet down"

We smell too much
 like a well-watered life
our roots pull forests
out of shadows

From nothing
we carve our world
into everything

Honesty can be cruel

some days it sets fire to my skin
other days my flesh folds into a small country
intimidated by its own smoke

3 things my demons and I have in common:

We handpicked our own hell
We fought G-d and lost
We have forgotten our greatest power is love

the wounded healer

The Thirsty Lover

He sees my half moon mouth
and salivates through his eyes
his hands squeeze my breast
holding out tongue
for well water

I tell him
Come with all the thirst
the ones before me couldn't satisfy

with each scrape
and suck
He trims down my soul

more
more

... just a bit more

there

Now I'm all the empty he's ever wanted

Do you see them?

These women
leaking tree sap and nectar
hoping you'll
look into their eyes one day
and call them *lover*

-    *the women inside me*

At Least Undress My Soul
Before Breaking It

He turns me over like a leaflet
panting as he mounts the shivers of my body

He plants his manhood in my insides
calling out to G-ds with names he mispronounces

I know he is relieved
when he grunts my ethnic name
the way elders do when you've done something
unforgivable

His tone collapses against my chest
calling for me
but not *all* of me

Just the parts that fit best in his mouth

La Petite Mort

"Did you come?"
he asks

scanning the holes
of my face
for G-d's eyes

Don't stop

    until I moan
    from the places
    I fear most

Until I speak in languages
    neither of us know

Until my soul
    leaves the weight of body
    behind

Gone Missing

Signs you have lost yourself

1. You stare water in the eyes and jump at your own reflection
2. Your heart is a storage house instead of an overflowing river
3. You've forgotten how to shed fruitful skin

Words

Use your tongue and carve my soul out

Run rosewata down my scalp

Caress blessings along my forehead

Touch me

Touch me in places
hands can't reach

Cowrie

The last boy who held his head between your legs
told his friends of what he saw

He never knew rosebuds tremor when watered

That some women hold the weight of oceans in their belly

That some wombs say

Come in
Take your shoes off
Stay forever

Your hands are a soft weapon
sanding down the armor of my body
My breath molds into a quiver as
a warm roux gathers on my panties

I see why grandma never used measuring tools

"It takes intuition to make gumbo
You just gotta feel your way around"

onion peel on the counter
my skin undresses in layers
soul first
heartbeat second

bay leaves
we prick our fingers and write love spells in blood

okra under our tongues
we are both hungry sticky things

burnt rice in the slow cooker
masking smell with smoke

2 parts tongue
1 part sassafras

We wipe down our simmer with
the soft of our mouths

The One That Got Away

Time comes with a sweat that bludgeons
that filths up our hair
and leaves cobwebs in every nook

Never take her for granted
says all who've taken her
wrath lightly

Look around
Time has turned many into souls
gasping for a breath to breathe

We may crown her *King*
but a day will come
when she leaves her throne behind

Your kisses stain my mouth closed

They remind me of damage
of things that kill slowly
of things that start gentle yet end up unholy
&
after youth has its way with my lungs

Will you still be here?

Him

I can tell your lips have been places I've begged them not
to go

Your words slur into apologies as
the scent of jasmine leaks through the phone

You stutter through the static:
"I'm sorry
she has a scent that just doesn't leave my bones"

Kitchen (1983):

*F*ufu warm on the counter
The folds of my eyes are wet with tears

wrapped in a cloth blanket
I am a shadow too small for my own clothes

the plantains are rotting
I eat my whispers alone as you dine on the fruit of her skin

dishes in the sink
I'll scrub my soul clean of you
even if I must get on my hands and knees

the house goes quiet
I pick myself off the floor

The Wounded Healer

Tell them how

    my fingertips mended your bones in place
    yet you ran off anyway
    panting the name of a new lover

Wata

Bringing you back to life

was a thankless task

chasing demons away
blowing warmth into your cells
planting kisses on your forehead

All for what?

I was the holy water they begged for
but never had the mouths to drink

The Hunger

When I saw his face
my eyes went hungry

"Where is the rest of him?"

Did he not see the marmalade I pulled from my thighs
the years I churned into memories
mornings of honey biscuits soaked in grits

When Life struck lashes at his spine

I came with earth and soft touch
and rubbed poultice down his back

I'll never understand

why G-d gave wings to
men who lift their feathers
not to fly
but to poke their sight out

Fangs

At times
I touch my skin
and still feel you there

This is the betrayal
of carrying a body that craves
what hurts it most

I may tremble

as I ask you to leave
So listen to my eyes instead

They'll say
"I never gave you permission
to make a home out of me"

If you are still confused
glance towards the wide of my growl

My teeth are
empty bellied
and waiting for the taste of blood

I warn you
My words can brand holes in your body

Once I release the wolves
there is no turning back
these lips are rabid and ready

Tell Anger

When she's good and ready
I'll be here

With rosebuds
and bottles of brandy
We'll soak   in the   infusion   for six weeks
        [sulk]   [confusion]

Smear our faces with relief and aloe vera leaf

Cool down, sis
is our chant

Our pores will flare open
            gasping as they utter their first breath

The Exorcism

We anoint her in *rosewata*

caressing past lovers out of

her hair
her pores
her moon

Once their
memory has left
she will be anew
and go by another name

Facial Profiling

If you could feel me through those trembling hands
I'm gentle to touch

If you could see me through those piercing glares
I'm feather stitch and cotton fluff
When innocence isn't busy
she wears my face too

Touching Glass After Hours | Jail Visits

I ask how he passes the time

He points at the graves in his eye sockets
Each of them dug
with knuckle and bare feet

He tells me he's cursed
and still
all I want is to hold his lips in my mouth

(I remember his taste
and the way it licked my wounds clean)

He bends me over in his mind
counting the stretch marks on my skin
one by one
until the voices in his head go quiet

the root work

Igbo Landing

H eaven:

Did you come with enough tear to drown those eyes?

A ncestors:

We have more tears than we can carry
Look at how our children are drowning above ground!

Elders say

    the free fall is harder than the landing

    that the true journey is finding yourself
    on the way down

Our soft palate was the first continent taken from us

It saddens me to know that our words once had a
homeland
that even they were stolen from

Questions

Who am I when the lights come down?

> When the floorboards fall undone?
> When life is a spirit too heavy to hold?

Grandpa v. Jim Crow

Grandpa slept in trees during the revolution
(one of two reasons why his enemies called him *monkey*)

A warrior fighting two wars needs twice the rest

with his third eye open
and a rifle in both hands
he was ready for anyone

"If they lynch me
 I'mma at least pick out the tree!"

Grandpa shuffles a deck of tarot cards

He lays the first card in front of me:
Hanged Man

We both let out a laugh

"They tried,
Good Lawd, they certainly tried
If they could they'd send lynch mobs after our souls too!"

Second Card: Magician

"Yea, I still have some tricks up my sleeve" he says

My eyes glance towards the sword bulging out
his veins

Heirloom

Forgiveness?

I don't remember when we last met but her name sounds
familiar

Does she wear our face?
Does she carry cayenne under her tongue?

Tell her if her eyes hang low
don't come here

We are not that kind
We new type omen
We a new type of woman
Stained teeth and hot breath
Last Name: Reparations
First Name: Collect

Who is forgiveness?
Whoever she is tell her our alchemy runs strong

We are Earth's bitter children
the ones who stood out in the sun too long

Break your mouth open
and speak freedom

Alternative Reality | Simulator

In your dreams

he looks healthy
refueled with all the energy life beat out of him

I've always loved you he says
I just didn't know how to show it

The eyes he wears are trembling
they can only hold his ego for so long

His lips quiver
and his face spills open like an avalanche

Your father is crying and he's never looked more
handsome

You hold his face in your hands

Lies

Your mouth = a scab for picking at

Your tongue = holder of soft words

Your teeth = more smile / less bite

Your chin = a place for fistprints

Is this what they said was the purpose of your face?

Who convinced you to go
to war with your own skin?

Wound Cleaning

Pulling damage from the root takes
the strength of a witch doctor

They know that pain outlives the body
that pain dances in a realm you and I never see
but we feel

Middle Passage (I)

S_{ea,}

Please release the bodies you swallowed whole

Lay them all ashore

I believe
I believe
I believe
they still have mothersongs to teach me

Middle Passage (II)

Y es

we survived
but did we come out whole?

EPSOM SALT & LAVENDER

Some people hold grudges until their fingers bleed
They touch themselves and wonder "Is this all I have left?"

"I'm a stranger in my own body" says Aunty
her calloused hands are soaking in a bowl of warm water

She picks at the ache in her scabs

"It gets tiring striking your own face
I want a softer touch
The one I had before the vultures came"

The Landfill of Bones

They never tell you when the
heartache leaves
or the work it takes patching your
breath back together

Our inner thighs bare thorns
Every person that has touched there has felt them

Baptise your hands in the folds of my skin

Can you feel it?
my belly is a landfill
of razor blades and shed kin

James spilled oil into me and set my hips on fire
he said he'd send for other village men to put it out

I kissed foam into Frank's mouth and his heart stopped
(He never used the silly thing anyway)

Nasir
plowed into me with club hammer and chisel

I showed his mother the holes on my body
"He'd *never* do that" she said

She repeats her words like an affirmation
burning her voice as she speaks

I suppose lies feel more honest
when you warm up the tongue

Weeping Through Moonset Eyes

The moon and I unravel
many nights together

She calls my scars
"womb marks"
hand carved with dirt and fingernail

We share an ancient pain
of dragging
memories across our backs

We are still learning
how to let
haunt sit within us
and not become us

Midnight presses her hooves into my skin
She fills my veins with nightshade
and rests flowers under my chin

Before midnight leaves,
I show her the stars she left under my eyelids

She holds my face towards the sky and says

Darling,
they were already there

Desire

Heaven caught you peeking
and now your bones crack out of place

Was it the lipstick stain on Eve's apple?
or the chills running down your spine?

Look at how we tear open your curse
and bathe it in palm wine

There is a name for us
and it's still unraveling
from our tongues

Remember us?
We are the moans
you couldn't bury alive

Milk

Motherland,

do you remember me?
I'm the daughter they pried from your hands

Standing in Our Power

Some days leave
without a forehead kiss goodbye

Other days
turn away at the sight of their own face

I sip wine slowly until twilight
drags me by the hair

Who left my skin in its place
when all I want to do is shed ?

My fresh skin will
stare lightning in the face
and yell
Try me

Some moons

must fight for their place
in the sky

1 + 1

There was once an angel
who folded their lips into a salve
and kissed me in places
only mouths could soothe

The angel came with wing and feather
and from the ledge
we jumped
together

It is true
We were our own undoing
but at least
we were brave

()

Did they not warn you?

I'm the wildfire you'll never see coming

I ooze
I spark
I pour into everything in my path

Get out of the way if you can't handle my smoke

When the ocean peels back her skin

her waves may arouse your interest
but never confuse her allure
as permission to enter

Daughter,

your beauty is no sanctuary
for the mouths of
hungry men

leave them in frustration

like salivating dogs
begging
for the chance
to swelter beneath
your sun

Beware fast talkers

they adorn you in the smell of rain
then take off running with your pulse in their hand

F-ck being the woman of your dreams

I am the warrior that haunts you
while you are wide
awake

Kintsugi

There is nothing like breathing through pain

The tantrums in my lungs
take their time
tickling my ribcage undone

My body is a storage house
with gold lining around its bones

When the storm came
me and debris
and broken bone
and broken bloodline
with bottle of moonshine
we made do
with the little air that passed through

We made do

the worship

Birth

The day I was born

floodgates fell from Heaven's mouth
and honey broke out everywhere

My mother pulled out her mother's tongue
and said

"My daughter's mouth is her sword,
let us see how she wields it"

On the 8th day,

Heaven and rain
fought over my name
The G-d with longer arms was crowned winner
The runner up hasn't been seen since

   -drought

*B*reathing was

my first revolutionary act

loving myself
was my second

Tools

Chisel off my shield

glide your hands
down
my soul scapes

taste what you find

To know heartbreak

without hardening
is to know peace

~~Earth:~~ *"The Small One"*

Our souls are too big for a body

Why do we small ourselves?
Did our past lives not teach us better?

Air: "The Calmer"

Take your time

and unwind with me

breathe into me as we
lay our wounds at the world's feet

Check in with your lungs
Do you feel them rising
& falling?

Look at us
We already have everything we need to grow

Fire: "The Movement"

You sit me on your lap
puffing cigar smoke in my face

You tilt your head and ask:

"Baaaaby,
        Baaaby
                who confused you for an ember?

I got a little somethin' for 'em"

You open your purse
revealing a revolver loaded with my teeth

Water: "The Weeper"

Emotions
ripple into wet

There is a reason why
I carry you
in places only lovers can reach

Earth is a crystal ball filled
of salt & you

A Reason for Love

Do it for the child in you

The one wailing
as the best
parts of you left
them behind

Forgiveness has water bearing hips

she comes in waves
swaying through fish markets
carrying a whiff of heart
an ounce of soul

When she

inches towards your breath
hold your head back

surrender
to the new voice
dripping down your throat

Rebirth

As I sleep my body nurses its wounds

My skin is an amulet I wear closely
Each night it replaces itself
with newborn soft

I'm not perfect
but I am my own healer

Everything I own
sits under my fingernails
dirty and rusty
but still mine

I carry
enuf lung for two lives
enuf drip for two skins
enuf water for three eyes

Honesty
when your soul spills
out of your mouth and
refuses to go back in

"Guarded people and plantains
have much in common" Ìyá Nlá says

Both browning
(but not rotting)

Both covered
(yet unfolding)

Both of soft flesh
(not gristle)

We scream a fit when thrown into the pit of love
but give us enough time
we'll come out golden brown and sweet on the tongue

If you want to know what freedom tastes like
open your mouth and close your eyes

Love Spell

The next lover of mine will have:

a face to get lost in

a soul bigger than their body

a love that teaches me
all souls can be mended
including
and especially mine

Heart Chakra Vol. I

I can tell by the shallow of your breath
that you've left your body

I open your chest
revealing sore spots
the safe places your inner child goes to hide

I pull out scrolls
entangled in cobwebs and watermarked with tears
Each scroll reveals the names of every lover and
unlover that left you

I stay there a lifetime

 and realize your name
is the only name written

If I tuck myself gently within your pores

will you carry me in your breath?

I don't mind being a throbbing feeling
a tremor you can't tame
a haven you flee to when the world slow drips into a
tsunami

Heart Chakra Vol. II

Phase I. Honeymoon

We play with each other's toes
counting the steps it took to get here

You look parched
like the journey took two lifetimes
and the sweat in your bones needs a moment to rest

I lay my hands on your heart
Is there room for me in such a trembling thing?
The most frightened part of you -
may I show you how to use it?

Phase II. The Real

I scared you away

didn't I?

Phase III. The Offerings

I send fruit to your home on the weekends

mushy cherries
you pull the stems by the hair

bleeding pomegranate
the seeds get caught between your teeth

juice of pineapple
it makes me taste *sweeter*

sun-dried mangoes
left out to dry since the day we first met

A day will come
when our fruit is picked by other people
We will call these *other people* lovers
We will call these *other people* better versions of ourselves

Phase IV. The Complete

I no longer ache when I think of you
this must be my body's way of
reclaiming its wholeness

Sankofa Breath

Rosewata,
I smell it on the center
of your tongue

It's not the only breath of yours
but by far
my favorite one

So come here
There's no sense in fearing love

The mothership is wedged in our mouths
So let's fly away
as dark matter
who never mattered here anyway

Eye 4c: The Vendor at the Trade Show

Her locs sway like
wind chimes
chanting good news
she calls them her "antennas"
laughing as she tells me her connection to G-d is so tight
her edges keep pushing back

She reaches across the table

handing me a sample of her botanical hair mask:
sunflower powder, volcanic ash, and moon beam

"Sis, *uncomb your heartbeat*
section by section
It gets easier, darling
Just add a little water
Smooth down each kink
Start where you are and
work towards the root"

\-   Fine tooth combing through life

Daily Regimen

Morning:

It's well over daybreak
and I haven't decided
which part of me to love

My eyes?
[the fortress]

My heart?
[the learner]

My mouth?
[the teacher]

Why choose
when all of me is worthy of wild love?

Nightfall:

Oil down your crown
　　lather off its scars
　　until its shine rivals the sunrise

Wrap a scarf around your head
　　until you look regal without trying

You are a special kind of divine
　　The kind that lingers
　　on the body and mind

Dream Journal - February 2040

I.

The walls were made of rose quartz
They were moving in towards me
ready to pierce my skin

The moment I surrendered
I woke up in a pool of nectar

II.

I twirl chants under my tongue
stumble over my voice
and get back up

These words feel heavy
these beautiful words I am coming home to

III.

Imagine a plant with roots bursting out of the soil

look at how it outgrew the pot you put it in

It sucked the water
flowing from your lips
closed its eyes
and
imagined itself as a sun
that rises
anyway

It never needed our faith
to sprout green flesh
and thick roots

That's the beauty of
believing in yourself

All you need
is you

I come to my altar

    Broken and
    Breathless

and somehow leave
smelling like something other
than a damaged woman

Before the Throat Chakra Could Speak

Four uses of their tongue:

- chasing welts down my back and ...
- folding their mouth into a fairytale and ...
- pulling nectar from my pores and ...
- finding my sweet spot and never leaving it

You are the wolf

howling the moon into fullness
tell us what you hear from the spirit realm

We are here to listen

- G

Sweetgrass Basket Mouth - A Dedication

You smell us
We carnal skin
We more hue-man than dryland could handle

We carry the scent of a thousand sirens

All us backwater swamp folk
with our backwash breath
toke air into our body bag lungs

It must hurt to see us this free
It must hurt to see who we be

So Gullah Geechee

How to [S]cry

I never thought
greatness could wear my face
until I looked into a mirror

Anointed

Tell me about the day a swarm of hummingbirds
drank nectar from your skin

Show me the homes they built with your hair and
the freedom songs they weaved into a nest

They still have not left,
have they?

Water Lily

Your fingers walked into my ocean and came out the
moon
shiny and glistening a scent of fresh bloom

There was a longing between
my thighs
and you knew

So keep the water running, honey

I want to spill over

Plenty Plenty

Y_{eye}
squat birthed rain then
carried on plucking flowers

the rain came with a smile

her harvest, plenty
her burdens, plenty
her scars, plenty

yet she still came with a smile

A Love Supreme

I'd tame my heart

but she's wiser than most

She survived me
carved a eulogy on my chest
that read:

"I'm not for everyone
I'll return when you give me what I deserve"

I was her flawed yolk

of skin folk
who loved despite all love had put her through

Empath

You wore
their wounds beautifully
but they were never
yours to keep

Protect your tears

they are
silent spells

what better way
for your body to heal its sadness
than to leak elixirs for the heart?

Some mornings I undress my skin

carry my wounds to the ocean
and watch them drink the sea for hours

Two Truths and a Lie

I.

The heart of heaven holds
  an ache only goddesses can mend

II.

When your tongue meets mine
  you'll know what sweetness tastes like

III.

Love is all I need

Jemima

This silk pouring down my chin carries her own shake

She is a free flow of tongue
a backwash of dreams
pouring back
to the sun

Did I mention my skin?
the sun-kissed robe
falling at my waist

My hills
overflow
with nectar-drenched pores

I am an
intimate sweat of
half sweet
and half supple
in one body

Mother Songs

It's first Sunday and I've finally worked up the nerve to
ask Grandma some life questions

Does love leave and come back stronger?
Will she leave a mark every time?

Grandma lets out a full-fledged smile

She too has been brimming with questions
only life has the throat to answer

Grandma replies -
Why is she called love anyway?

Love should be called war paint
Look at how she scares these cowards away

The stains love left on your skin
They are just reminders of what you two have been through
Darling, can you blame her
Who else could wear love so beautifully?

*Y*our lovers should look

into your face and find peace
Not for them to take
but for them to witness how blissful you can be without them

Grandma plucks her secrets
from the bottom of the ocean
and lays them into my hands

I wonder how life has not hollowed her out
How is she so filled with rebirth
that even the ocean overflows with her magic ?

The woman you are

The woman you're becoming
and the woman you used to be

Love all three
in equal measure

  -   *Holy Trinity Spell*

I.

While the world is asleep

we are just getting started with the use of our tongues

Our mouths are full and blushing
like primroses blooming in the nighttime

I press my fingerprints into Mom's belly
feeling for her empty

Where is the rotting? the shrapnel spleen?
the hollow home?

II.

Mom points at the cooing sounds pouring out of her
navel

Her stretch marks sing like thunder pouring from clouds

I lean over
counting each bolt of lightning
until the palm of my hands feel a light kick

III.

"We are witches. We only frighten people who are afraid of the truth"

our lungs
a breathland

our blood
saffron aged in whiskey

our spells
oozing from four lips

"The moon birthed us knowing we'd be too much for this
world

So who are we to question our greatness?"

IV. Time Capsule

The women travelled miles for water
with their firstborns tied around the small of their backs

Most returned with jugs of water on their heads
My mother returned with an entire river

V.

She opens her hand

revealing the thick of a
throbbing vein

"*My secret*, she says
is I grab life by the jugular"

The Ocean Who Drowned Half the World

Tell your children
you broke the sky open
just to pull them into the world

Heaven spat them out

screaming
"Now who will be here to awaken the angels?!"

Noon looks at me and says

Give freely
Give first

I used to ask why
Now I just look towards the blessings
falling off my shoulders
and into my hands

Don't let this world

beat
the empath out of you

My ancestors have been waiting

for someone with my strength
to carry their name

Nothing softens the wounds of your ancestors

like the sweetness of your existence

I.

We are all empty
and gasping for air

If the sun held a chalice
against your lips
would you sip from it and
taste your blood
pouring back into your body ?

II.

I scratch my skin like the base of a river

carving love into me until I look claimed

I've marked myself with the thing they told me I'd never
find ... myself

III.

Since God is here, I have a few questions to ask

May I lay my head on the ground and weep?
May I grow wings and use them?

May I fly, for just once, may I fly?

Last night

a soothsayer
said I would take my life
and
pull it
into a greatness
that would
make my shadow tremor
and ask

Am I worthy of following her?

F lutter Softly

in a world that seeks to harden you

Flawed women can be loved

in fact
we are the best women to love

All that your ancestors had to

go through for you to be here
and you doubt yourself?

How dare you

You come from a legacy of survival that must never be
questioned

Closing Ceremony

Use the energy generated from this reading experience
to write a note for someone you love

Yes, that someone can be you